THE READING HOUSE

This book belongs to:

rhcbooks.com

Educators and librarians, for a variety of teaching tools,
visit us at RHTeachersLibrarians.com

ISBN: 978-0-593-51618-8

Printed in China

10 9 8 7 6 5 4 3 2 1

First North American Edition

CPB/1800/2030/1121

Random House Children's Books supports the
First Amendment and celebrates the right to read.

Kindergarten Math

Contents

This is going to be **fun**!

Welcome to The Reading House

Marla Conn, MS Ed., is a reading and literacy specialist with a Master of Science in Elementary Education and Reading, and over 15 years of experience as a teacher in New York public schools.

During my years as a teacher, literacy specialist, and educational consultant, I have worked with hundreds of children and have a deep understanding of how the right books and instructional materials can provide rich, meaningful experiences that build a strong foundation for learning.

The Reading House was created out of the need to provide children with a comprehensive and systematic educational tool. It combines dependable strategies that have been proven to motivate, educate, and spark the process of learning, using an innovative storybook, character-based approach.

What began as a leveled learn-to-read program has grown into an entire educational universe, with materials to cover all aspects of early learning, in a variety of engaging formats. Each book in the series has been carefully devised and designed to inspire and encourage young children and adheres to the core principles and key building blocks of early learning.

Let's get **started!**

The Reading House is one-of-a-kind: an inviting, accessible, informative space where children can learn and grow. With its engaging cast of characters, bright and playful illustrations, and consistent setting, The Reading House is a world that early learners will love to return to, again and again.

I am so excited for children to get their hands on these books and to watch the lightbulbs switch on!

Happy Reading!
Marla Conn

Hints and Tips for
Parents and Guardians

Kindergarten Math supports kindergarteners in the development of the key mathematical and numerical skills they will need to be school-ready. Designed to be as enjoyable as it is educational, little learners are joined on their journey by the fantastically fun cast of The Reading House.

The activities in this workbook build upon the basic preschool concepts learned in **My First Number Skills**, introducing children to a more complex set of skills, including working with numbers up to 20, measuring, counting money, and telling the time. This workbook is the perfect companion for readying learners for their school ventures.

Before embarking on this exciting mathematical journey, there are a few hints and tips parents and guardians should bear in mind.

☆ HELP:

As you progress through the workbook with your child, help them by reading instructions aloud and explaining activities further. It's especially helpful to emphasize and repeat key mathematical terms. Practicing numbers orally is encouraged too, to improve familiarity with what your child is learning on paper.

☆ MANIPULATIVES:

To aid their developing mathematical skills, many children will benefit from seeing and handling physical objects, or manipulatives—items such as buttons or blocks.

☆ ANSWERS:

Refer to the answers section at the back of the workbook once your child has completed an activity. Ensure they fully comprehend the concept presented before moving on to the next activity.

⭐ WRITING INSTRUMENT AND GRASP:

By kindergarten age, your child is getting comfortable using a pencil as their hand muscles and fine motor skills are developing. It is helpful, however, to frequently reinforce ideal pencil grasp, per the following steps:

- Hold the pencil between thumb and index finger, with index finger on top.

- Rest the pencil on the middle finger.

- Rest the side of the hand comfortably on the table.

We love numbers in **Happy Town**!

⭐ FORMATION:

This workbook uses a system of dots and numbered arrows to demonstrate the correct formation of characters.

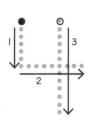

- ● The black dot indicates the starting point for the pencil.

- → The arrows show the direction of pencil movement, and should be followed in numerical order.

- ◎ This additional dot indicates that the pencil should lift off the page to make a separate stroke.

⭐ WRITING LINES:

This workbook uses writing lines consisting of three lines with a dotted center to encourage proper character formation.

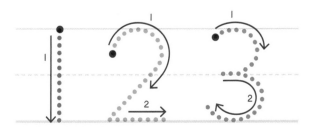

Trace and **write** the **numbers** as words and numerals.

zero 0 0 0

Practice here:

one 1 1 1

one

two 2 2 2

two

Practice here:

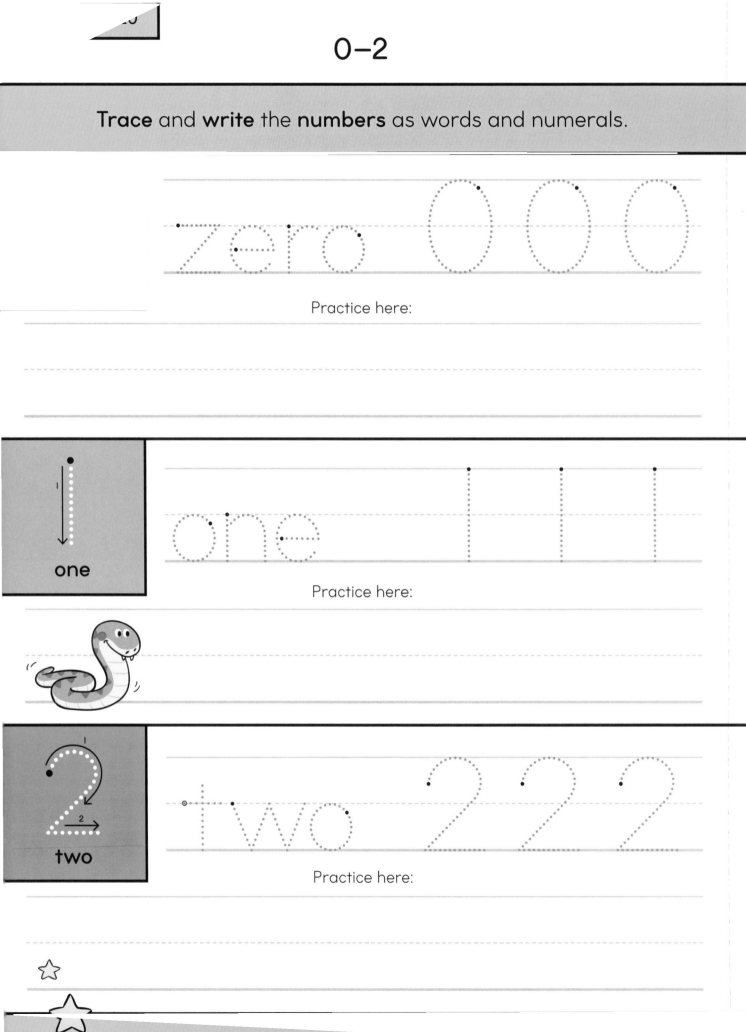

Continue all the way up to **20**!

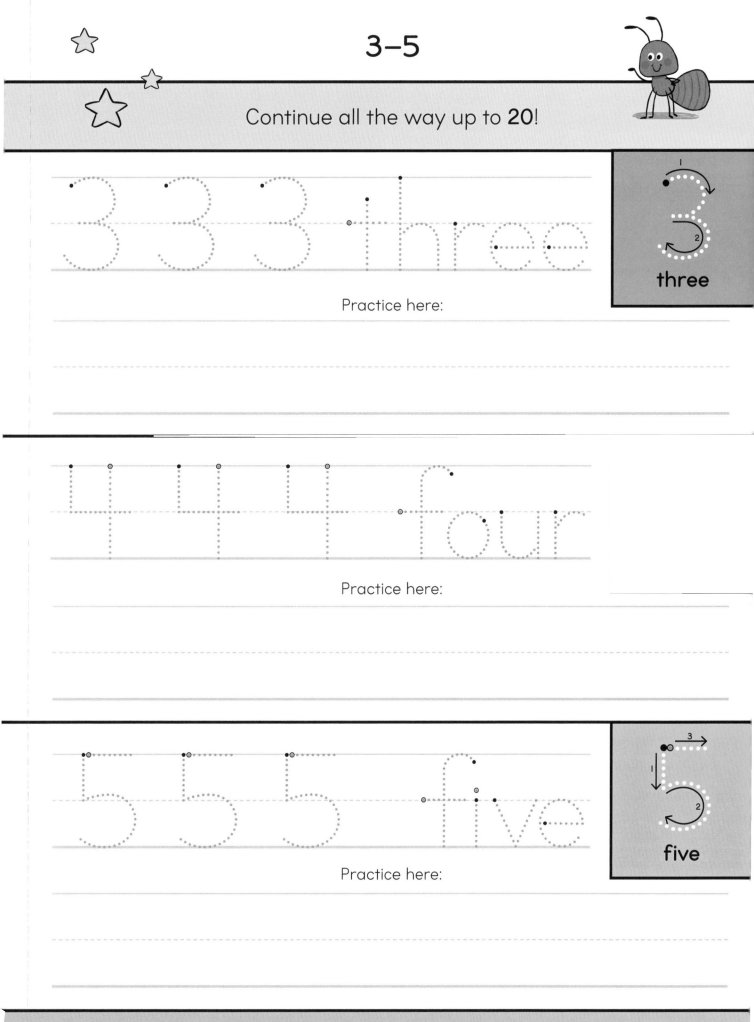

3 3 3 three

3 three

Practice here:

4 4 4 four

Practice here:

5 5 5 five

5 five

Practice here:

6-8

six

666

Practice here:

seven

seven 777

Practice here:

eight

eight 888

Practice here:

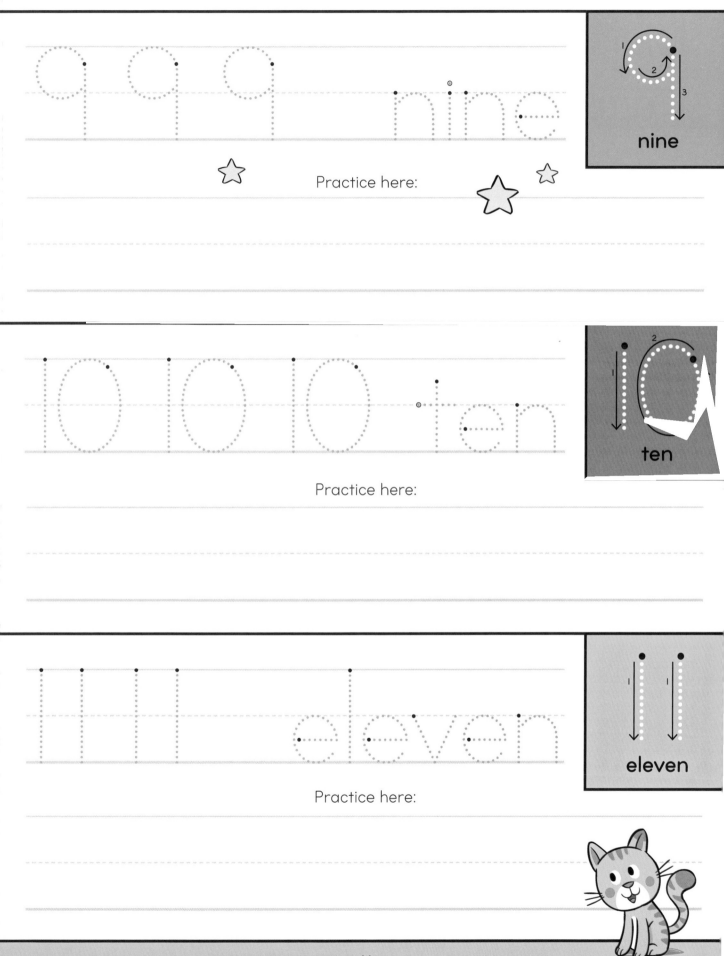

9 9 9 nine

nine

Practice here:

10 10 10 ten

ten

Practice here:

11 11 11 eleven

eleven

Practice here:

12-14

twelve 12

Practice here:

thirteen 13

thirteen 13

Practice here:

fourteen 14

fourteen 14

Practice here:

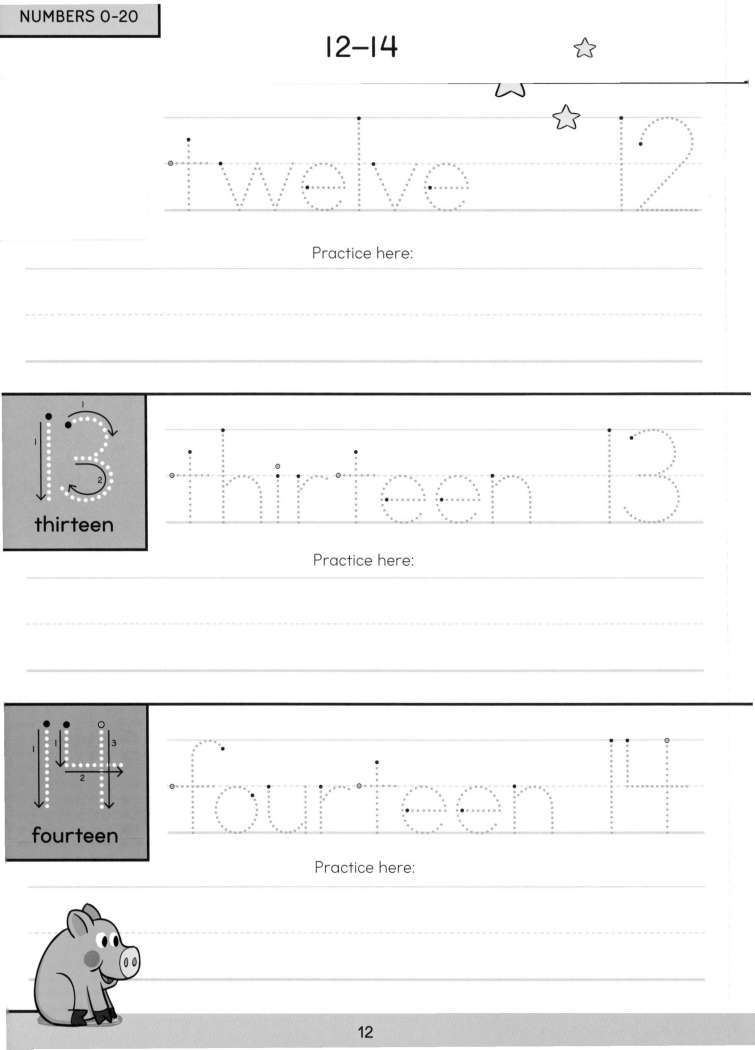

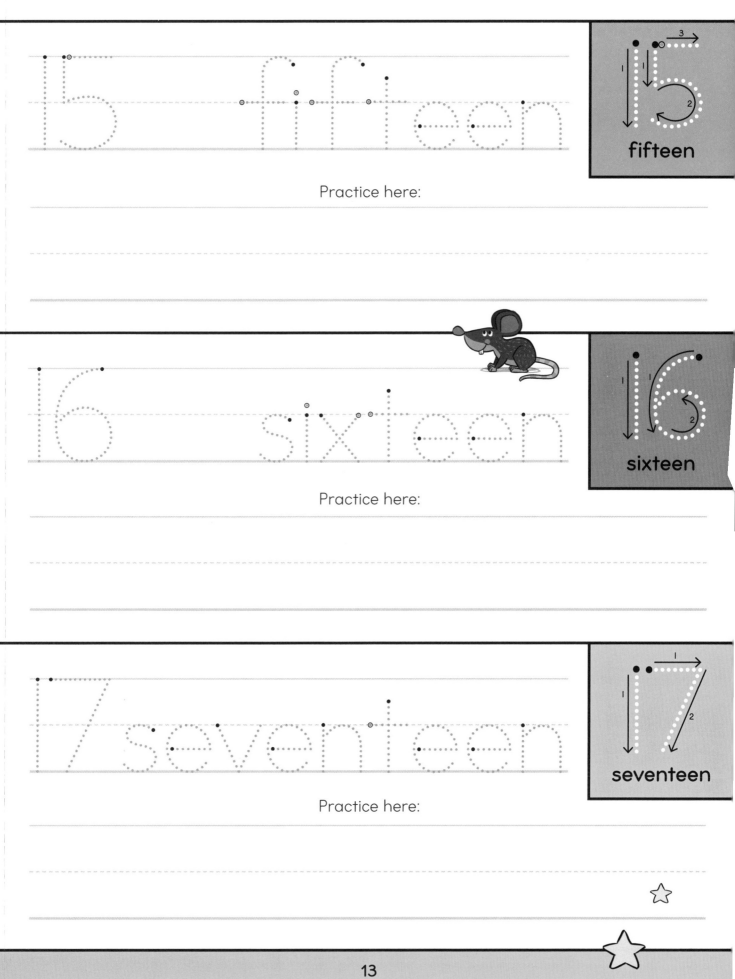

15   fifteen

fifteen

Practice here:

16   sixteen

sixteen

Practice here:

17   seventeen

seventeen

Practice here:

18–20

eighteen 18

Practice here:

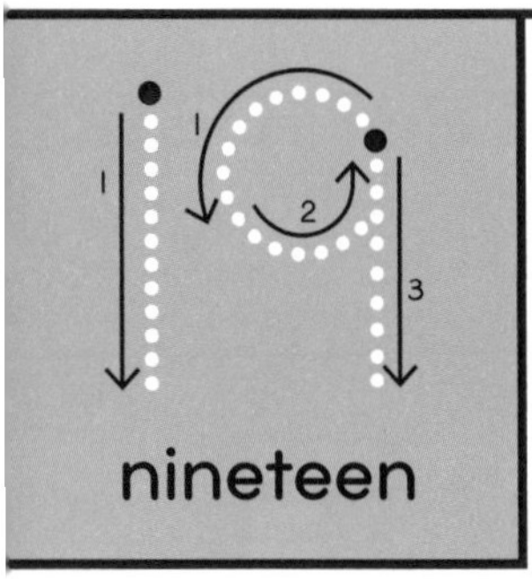

nineteen

nineteen 19

Practice here:

twenty

twenty 20

Practice here:

Number Match

Draw lines to match the **numerals** and **words**.

0
1
2
3
4
5
6
7
8
9
10

four
nine
ten
seven
five
two
zero
one
six
three
eight

11
12
13
14
15
16
17
18
19
20

eighteen
sixteen
nineteen
twenty
fourteen
eleven
seventeen
twelve
thirteen
fifteen

Counting Forward

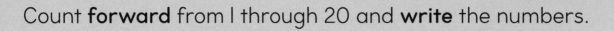

Count **forward** from 1 through 20 and **write** the numbers.

1

20

Counting Backward

Count **backward** from 20 through 1 and **write** the numbers.

20 →

1

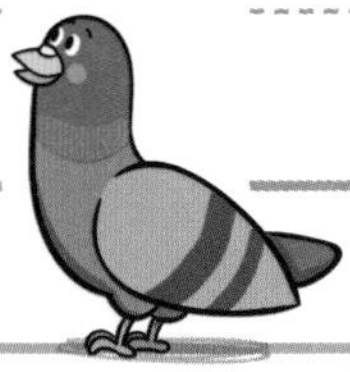

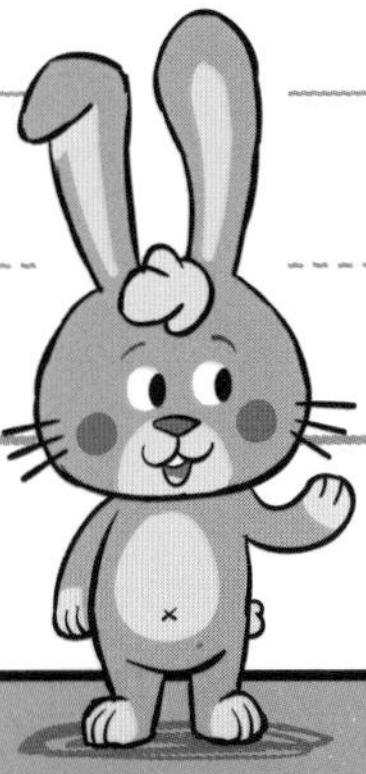

Forward Sequences

Write the **numbers** that are missing in these **forward** sequences.

1 2 3 4 5

___ ___ 13 14 ___

5 ___ 7 ___ ___

___ 3 4 5 ___

___ 15 ___ 17 ___

Backward Sequences

Now, try these **backward** sequences.

5   4   ___   2   ___

___   9   8   ___   6

5   ___   3   2   ___

15   ___   ___   12   11

___   19   ___   17   16

Before, Between, and After

Write the number that comes either **before**, **between**, or **after** the circled numbers shown.

19 → 20

3 →

← 16

← 6

12 → ← 14

1 →

16 →

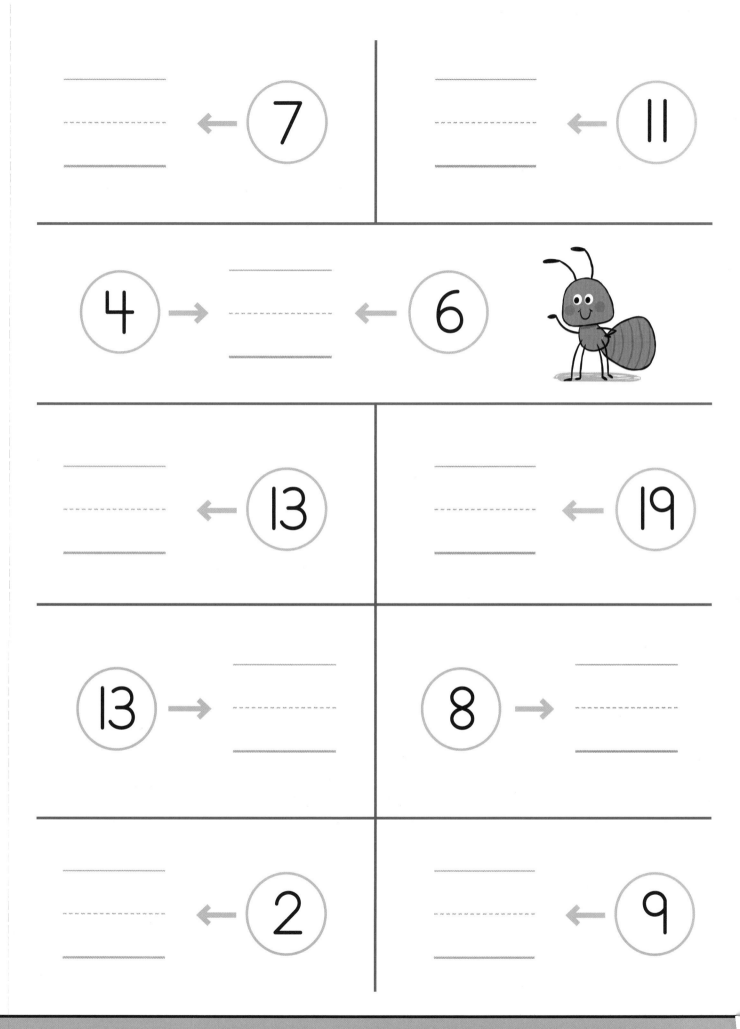

7 ←

11 ←

4 → ← 6

13 ←

19 ←

13 →

8 →

2 ←

9 ←

Count and Color

Count the dots. Then, use the answer key to **color** the picture.

Count and Write

Count the objects and write the total number.

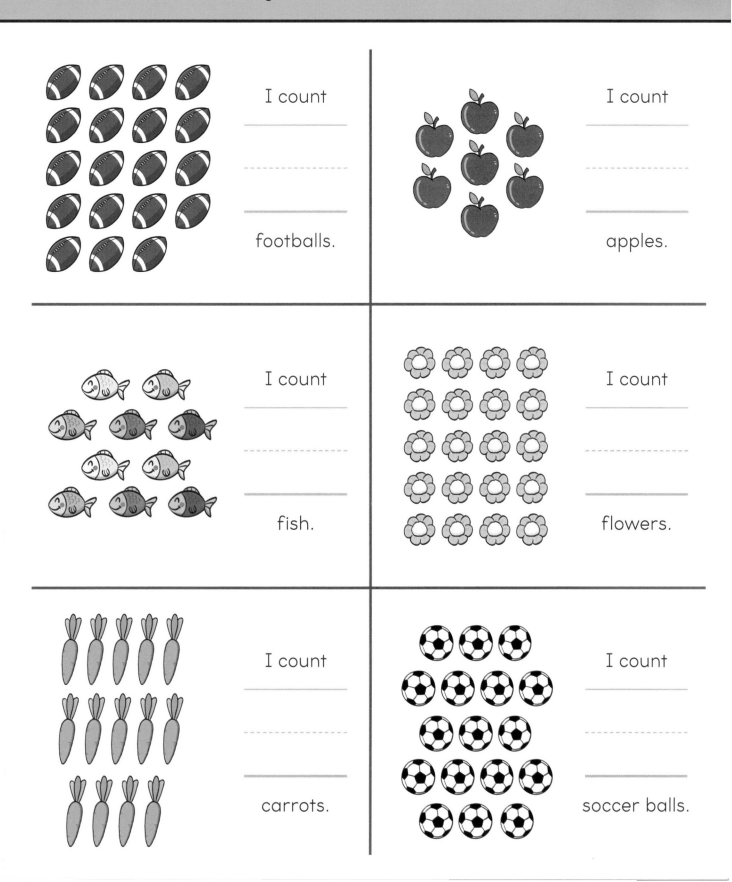

I count

_____

- - - - - - - - - -

_____

footballs.

I count

_____

- - - - - - - - - -

_____

apples.

I count

_____

- - - - - - - - - -

_____

fish.

I count

_____

- - - - - - - - - -

_____

flowers.

I count

_____

- - - - - - - - - -

_____

carrots.

I count

_____

- - - - - - - - - -

_____

soccer balls.

Counting by Tens and Ones

tens	ones
1	2

tens	ones

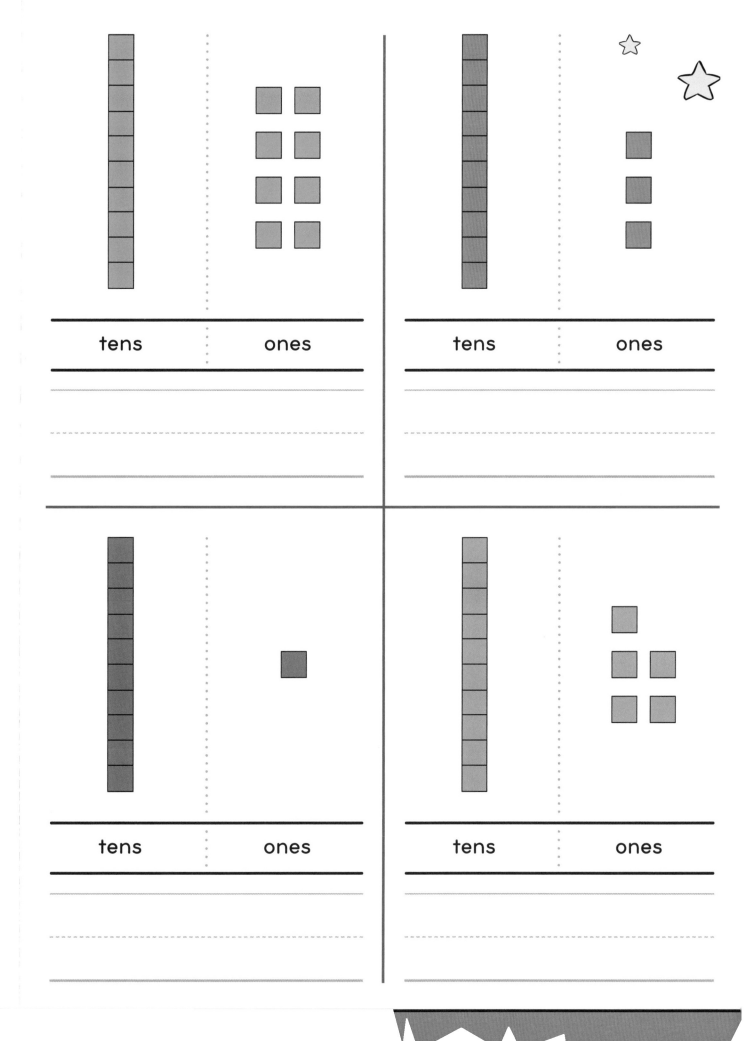

tens	ones

tens	ones

tens	ones

tens	ones

Skip Counting by 2

Count by **2** and write the **missing numbers** in the boxes below.

2 6

Skip Counting by 5

Count by **5** and fill in the **missing numbers** on the gloves.
Use the numbers in the key to help you.

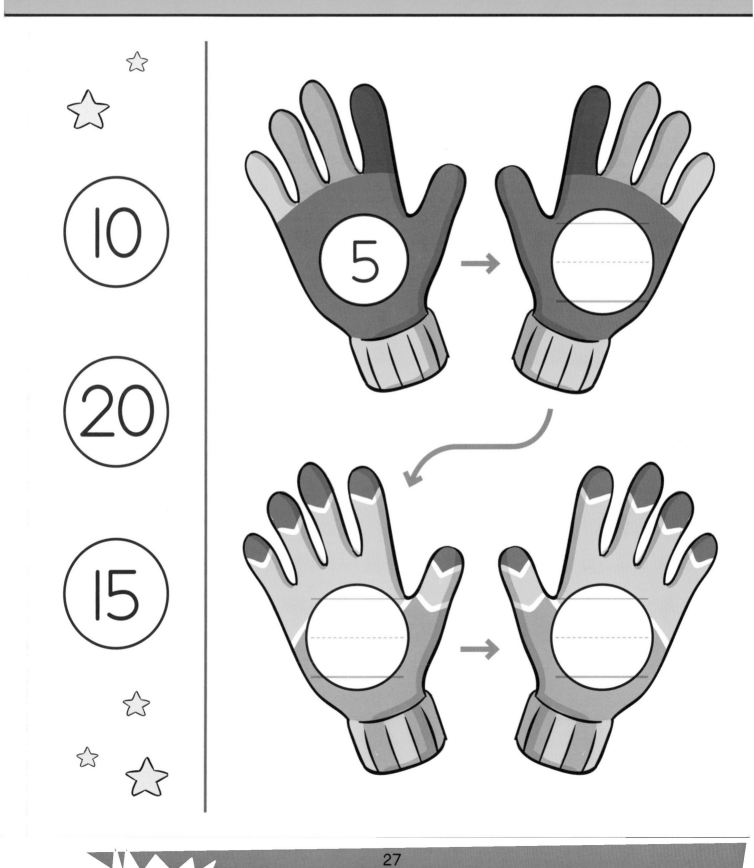

Skip Counting by 10

Count by **10** to help the animals find their way to **100** and **Zoo School**.

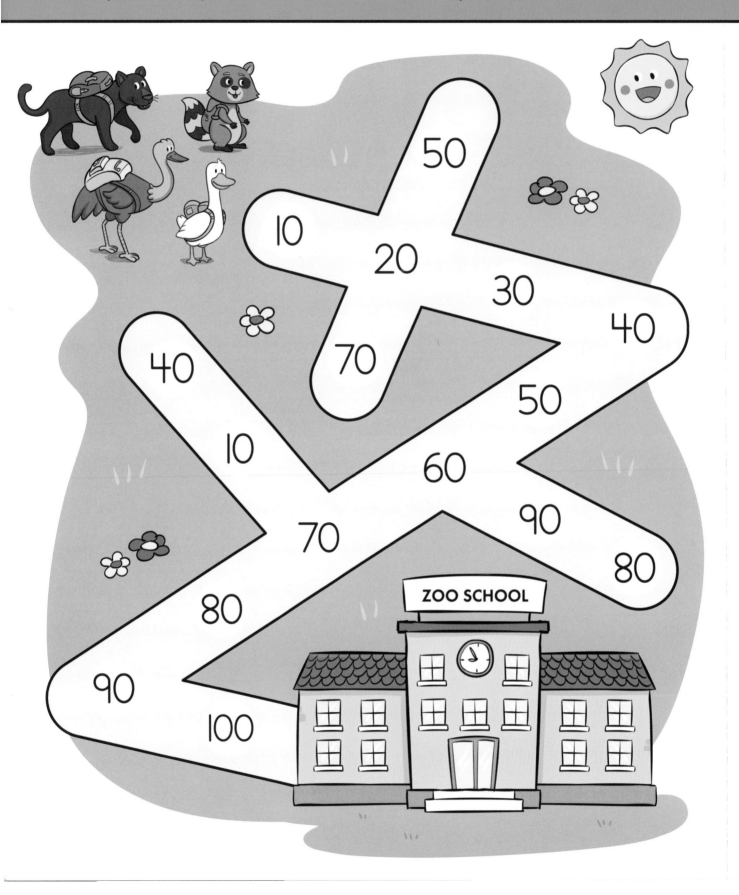

More Practice with Skip Counting

2 4 ___ ___

5 10 ___ 20

10 20 ___ 40

10 12 ___ ___ 18

More and Most

Count the objects and write the total. Circle the group in each row that has **more**. Then, find the one group on the page that has the **most**.

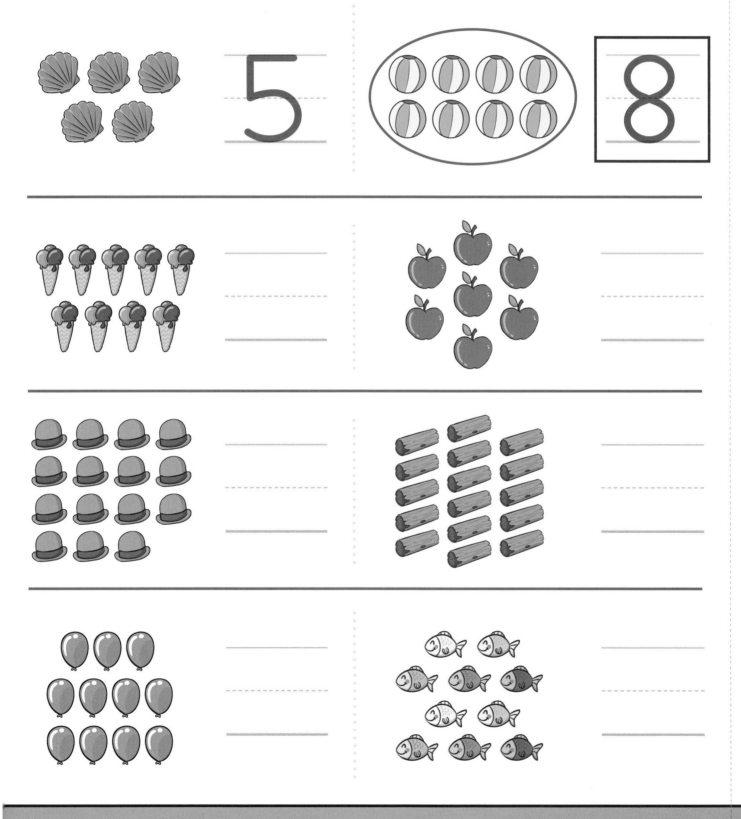

Count the number of **pens** and write the total.
Circle the group on the right that has **1 more**.

Count the number of **fish** and write the total.
Circle the group on the right that has **3 more**.

Count the number of **party hats** and write the total.
Circle the group on the right that has **5 more**.

Fewer and Fewest

Count the objects and write the total. Circle the group in each row that has **fewer**. Then, find the one group on the page that has the **fewest**.

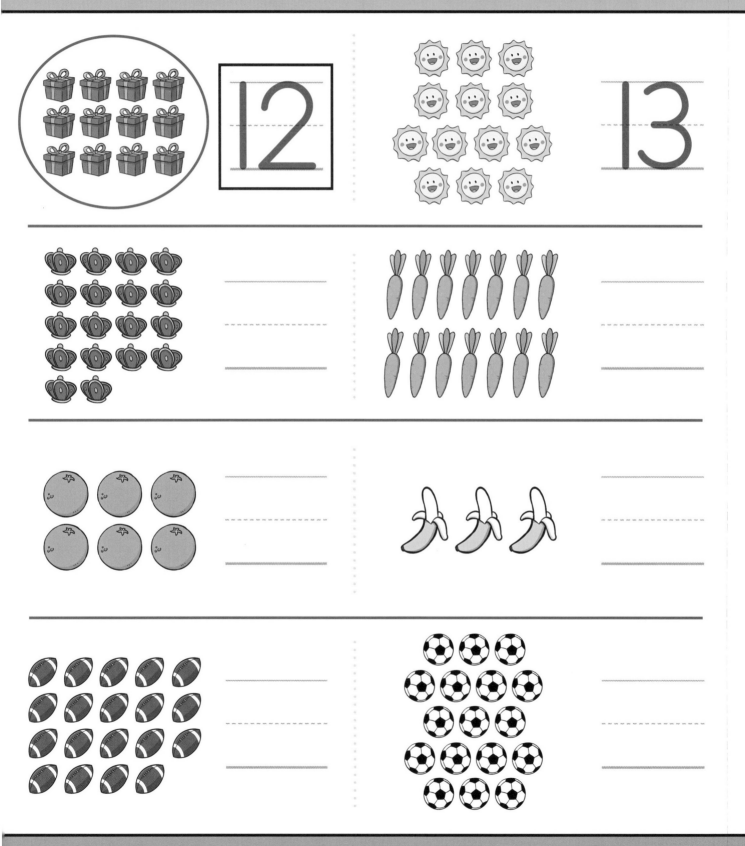

Count the number of **gifts** and write the total.
Circle the group on the right that has **2 fewer**.

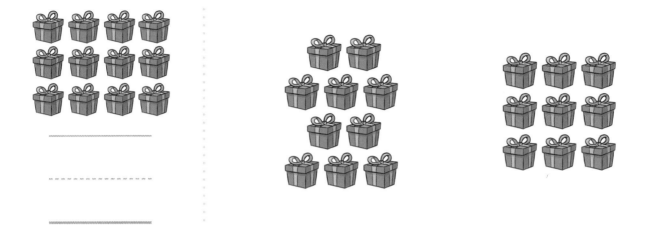

_____

- - - - - - - -

~~~~~~~~~~~~

Count the number of **hats** and write the total.
Circle the group on the right that has **4 fewer**.

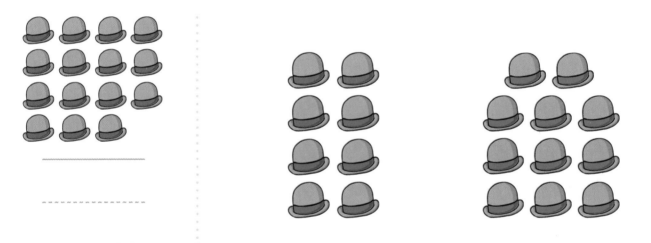

_____

- - - - - - - -

~~~~~~~~~~~~

Count the number of **fish** and write the total.
Circle the group on the right that has **5 fewer**.

_____

- - - - - - - -

~~~~~~~~~~~~

Number Bonds for 1–5

Let's review **number bonds** for 1–5.
Count the objects and fill in the circles.

A **number bond** is a pair of numbers that add up to make another number.

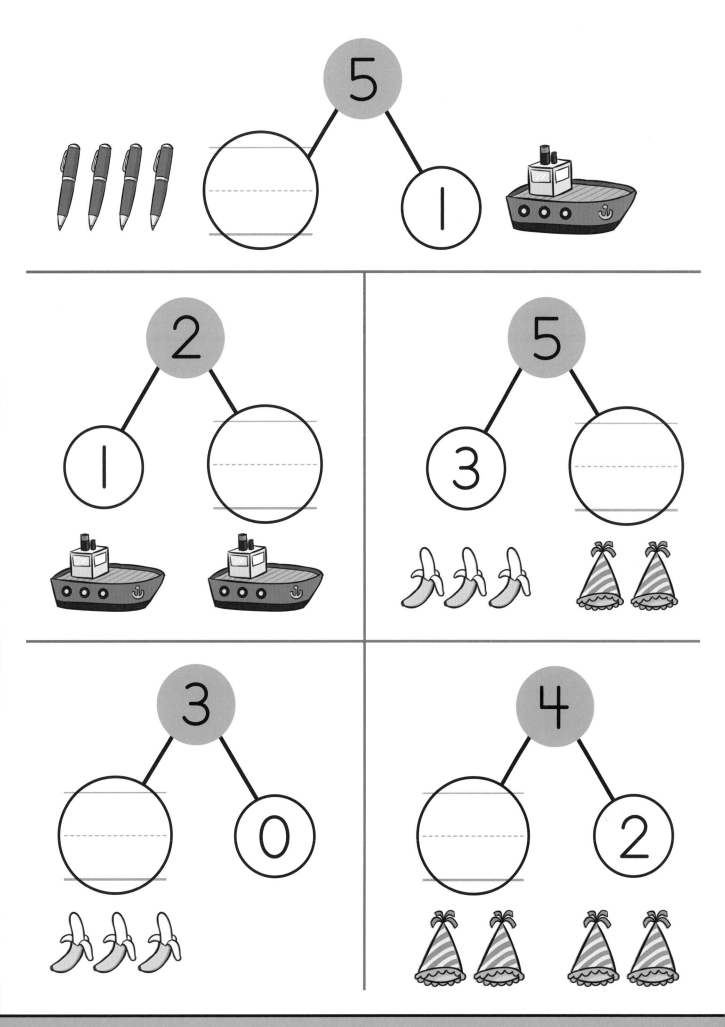

Number Bonds for 6

What do we need to make 6?

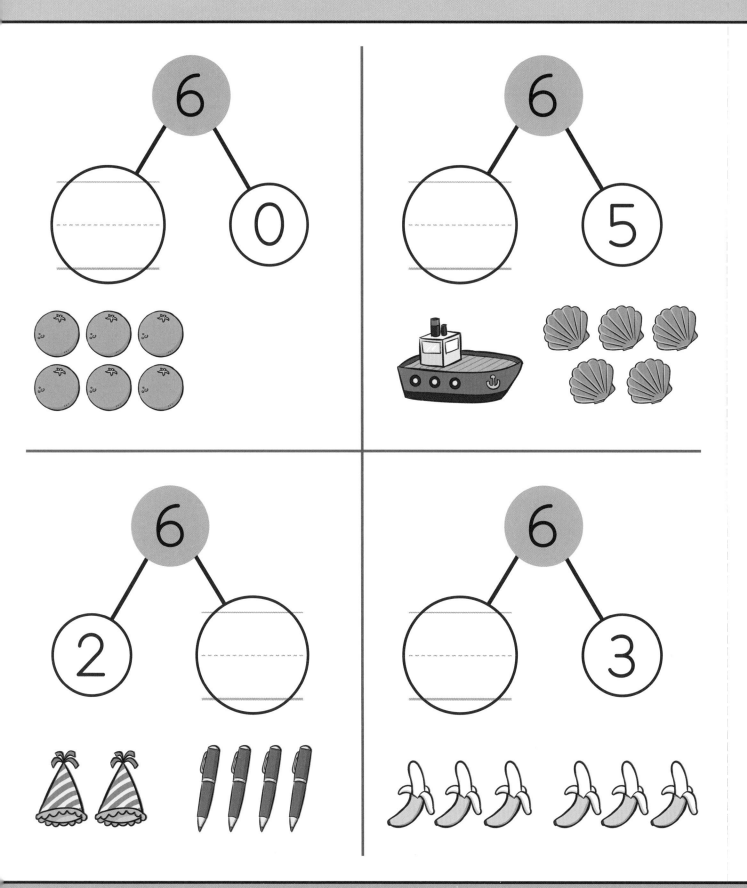

Number Bonds for 7

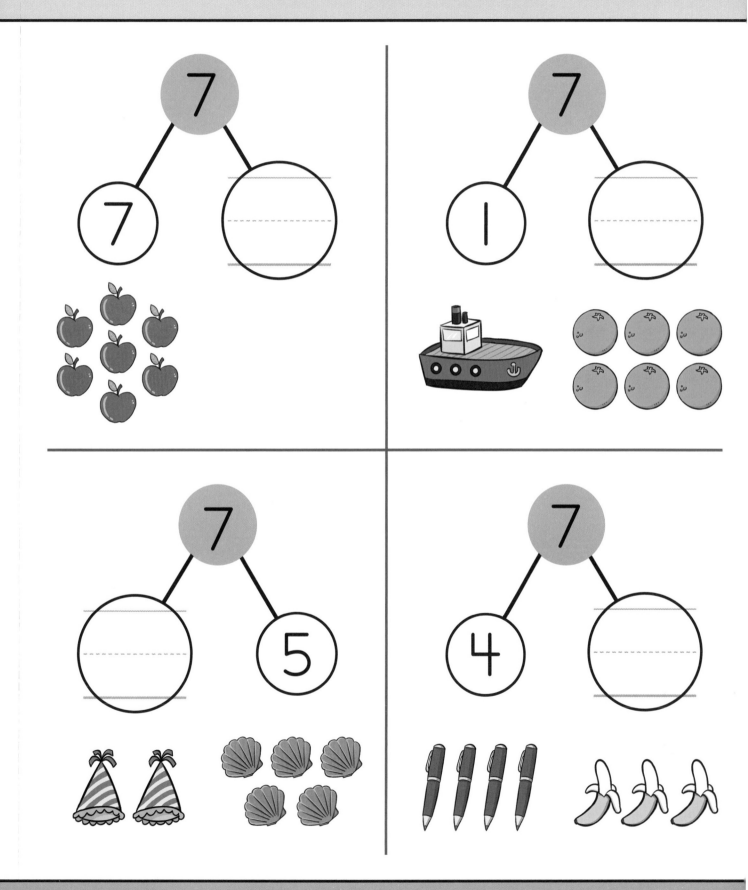

Number Bonds for 8

What do we need to make 8?

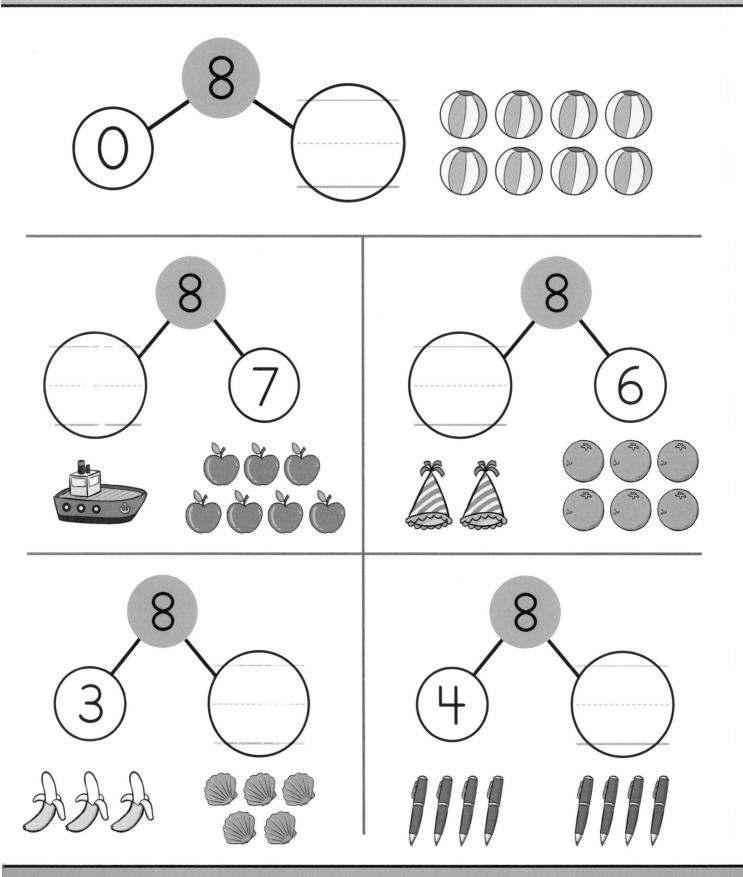

Number Bonds for 9

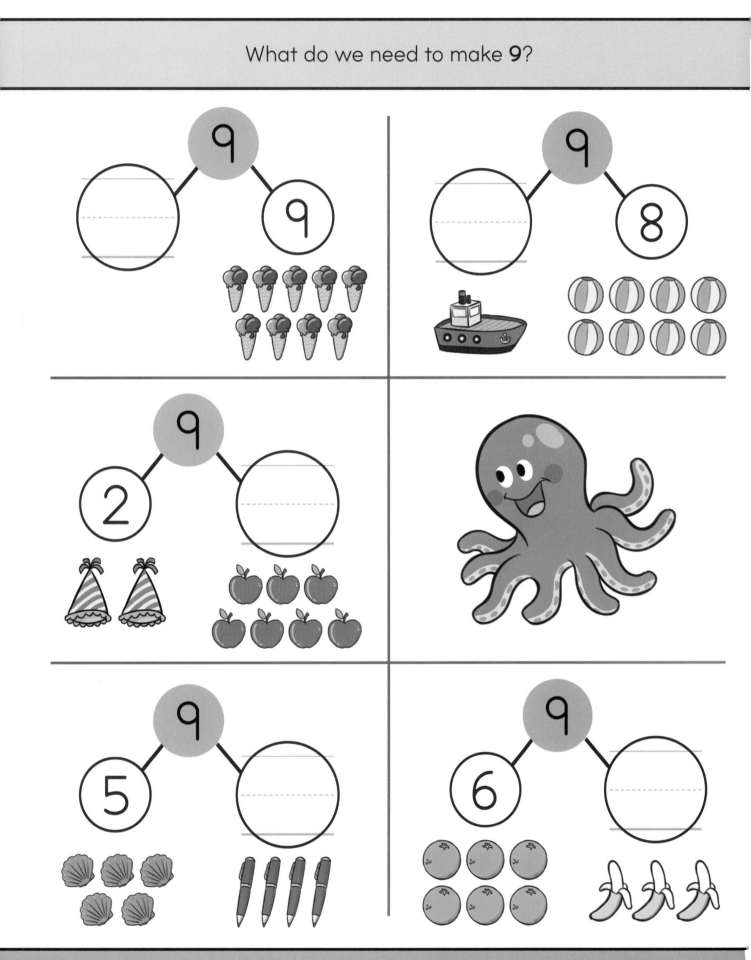

Number Bonds for 10

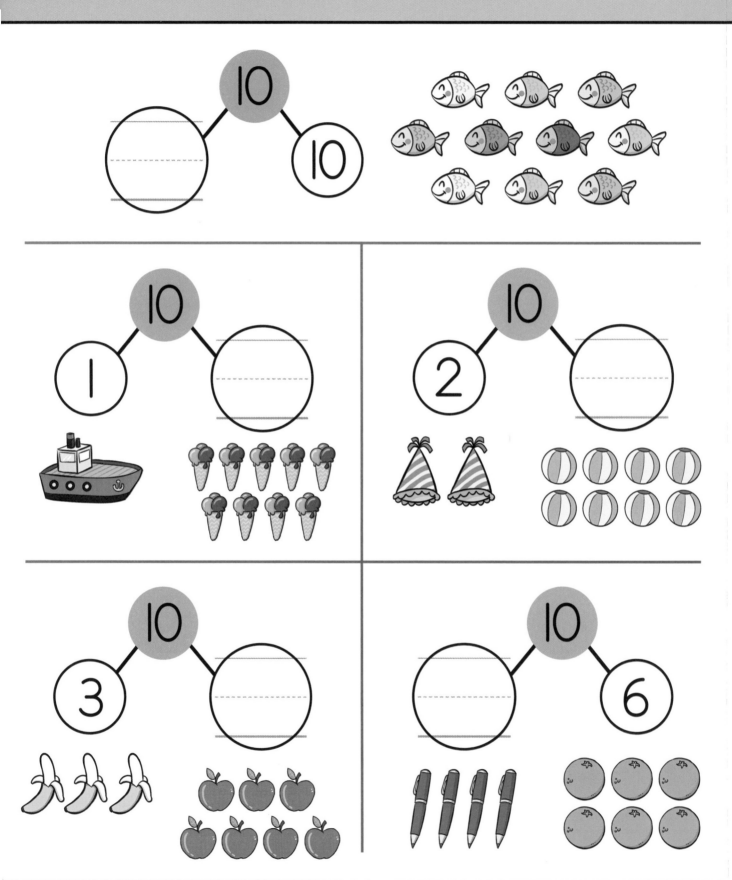

Number bonds help us with **addition** and **subtraction** skills!

41

Number Bonds for 20

What do we need to make **20**?

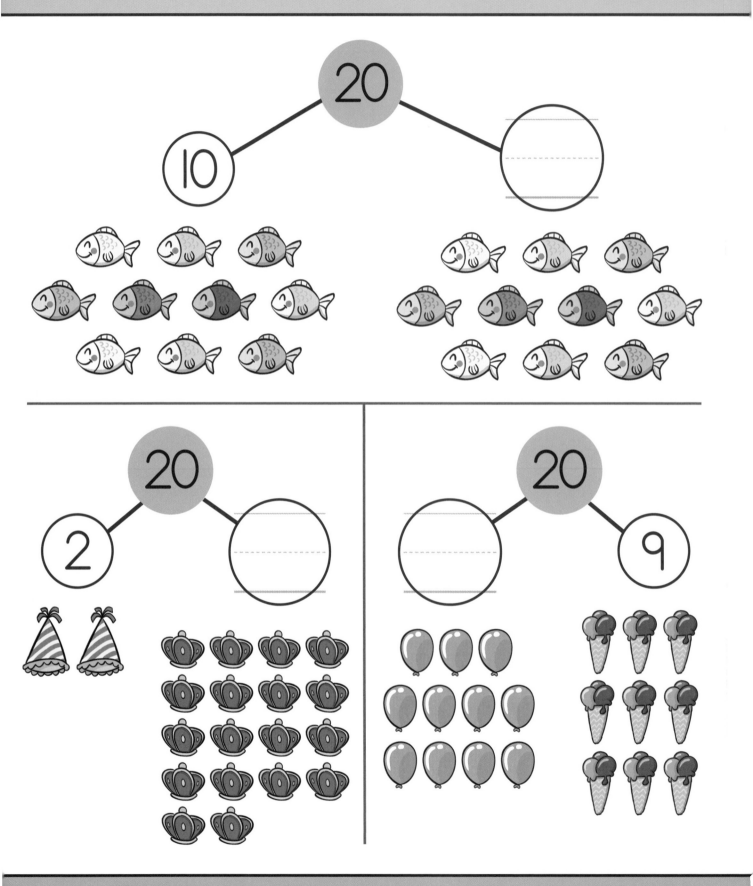

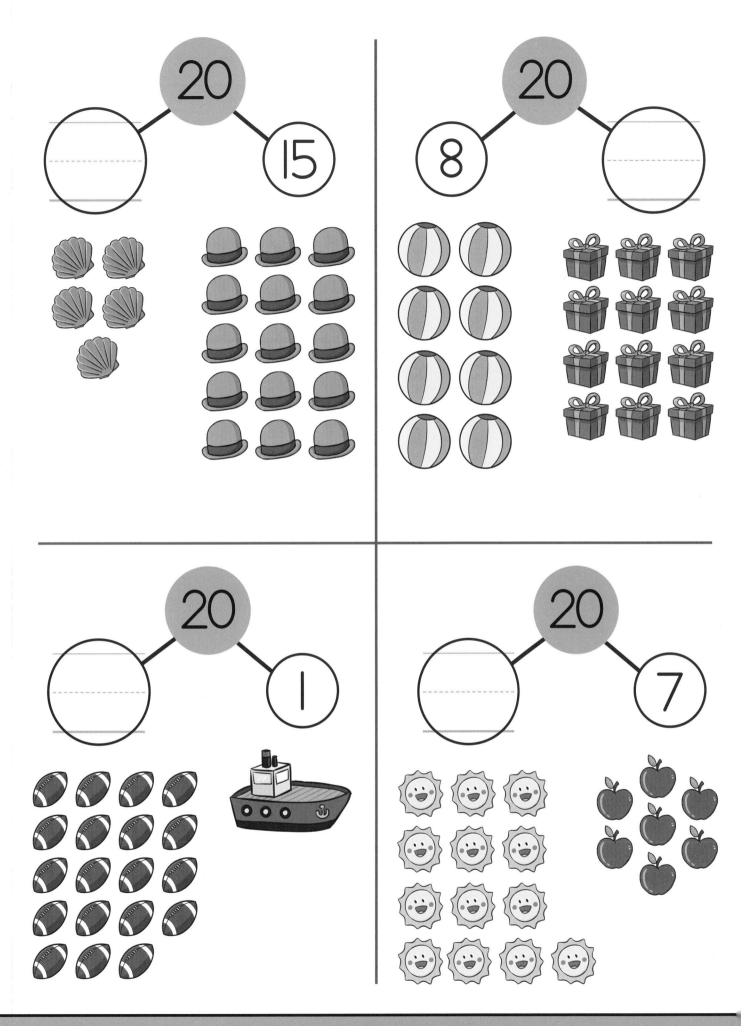

Addition

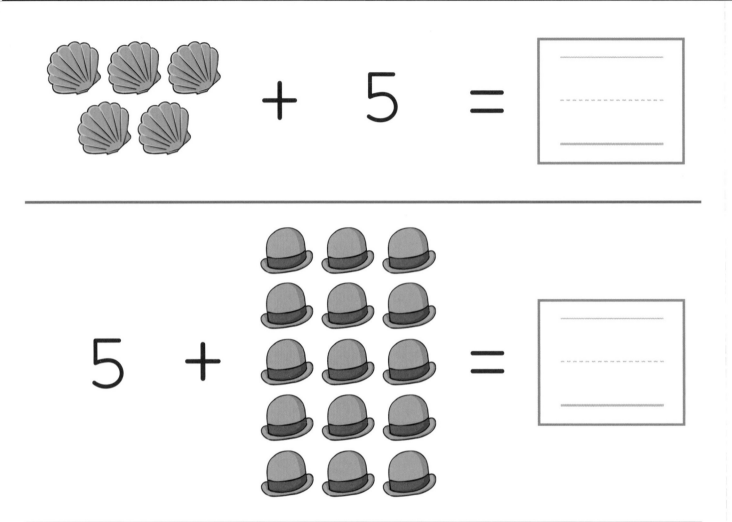

$+$ 5 $=$

5 $+$ $=$

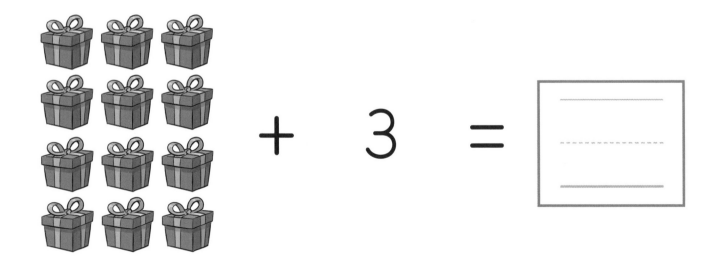

$+$ 3 $=$

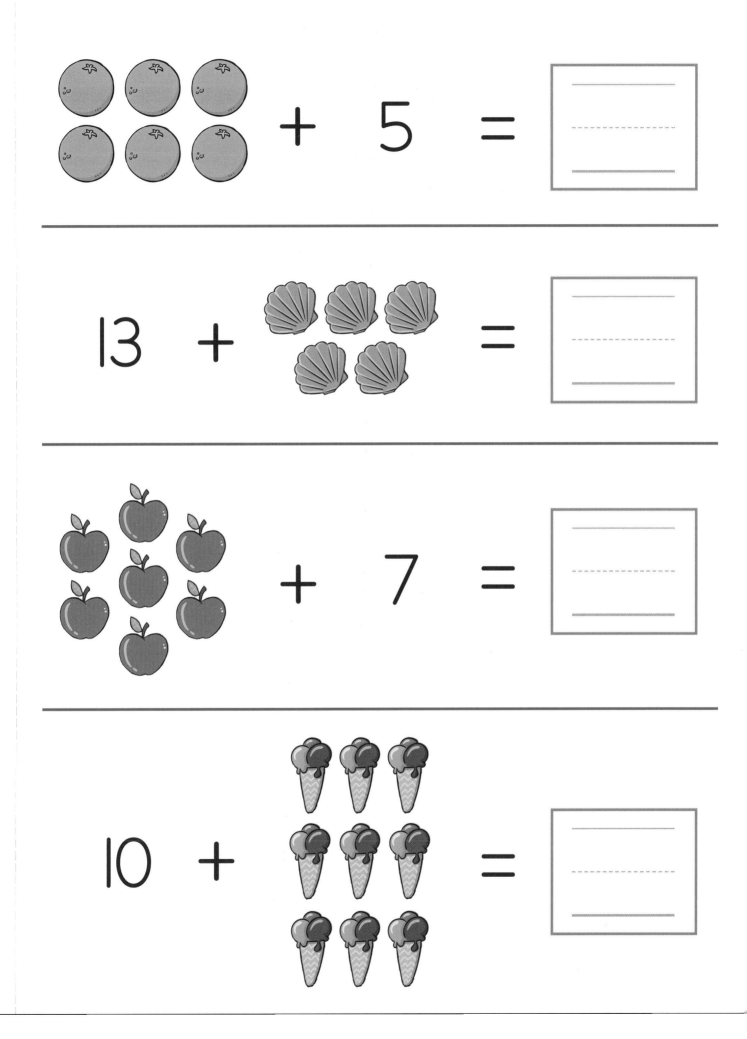

6 + 5 =

13 + 5 =

8 + 7 =

10 + 9 =

Color by Addition

Addition Maze

Find the **sums** and follow numbers **10 through 15** to reach the Chess Den.

4 + 6 =

10 + 7 =

1 + 11 =

7 + 4 =

2 + 2 =

10 + 3 =

3 + 11 =

4 + 12 =

1 + 16 =

8 + 7 =

10 + 10 =

START

CHESS DEN

FINISH

Subtraction

Count the objects and subtract the smaller number from the bigger number. Cross out the objects to help you. Then, write the total in the box.

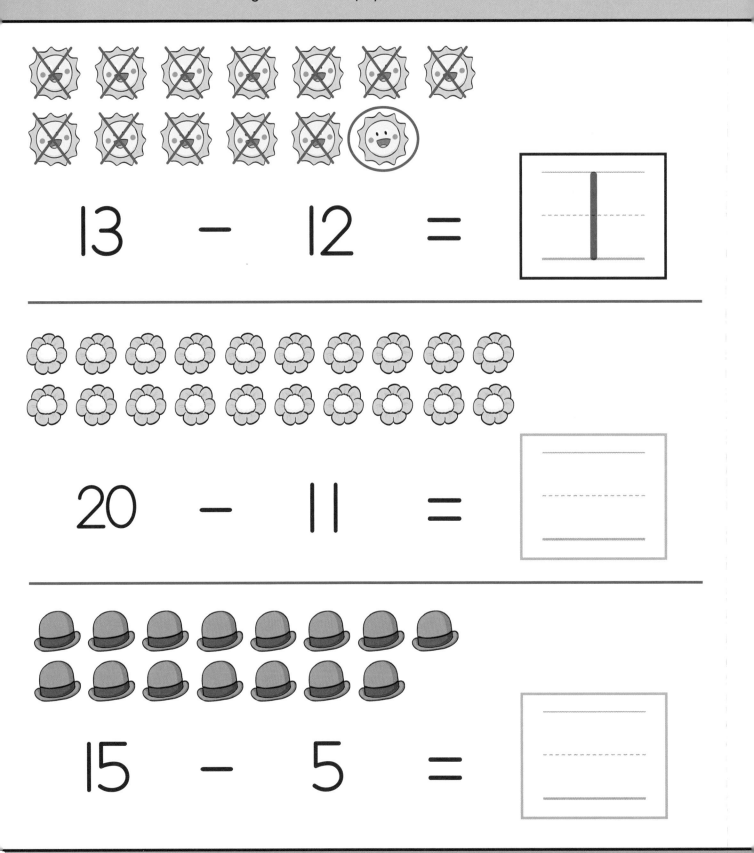

13 − 12 = [1]

20 − 11 = [ ]

15 − 5 = [ ]

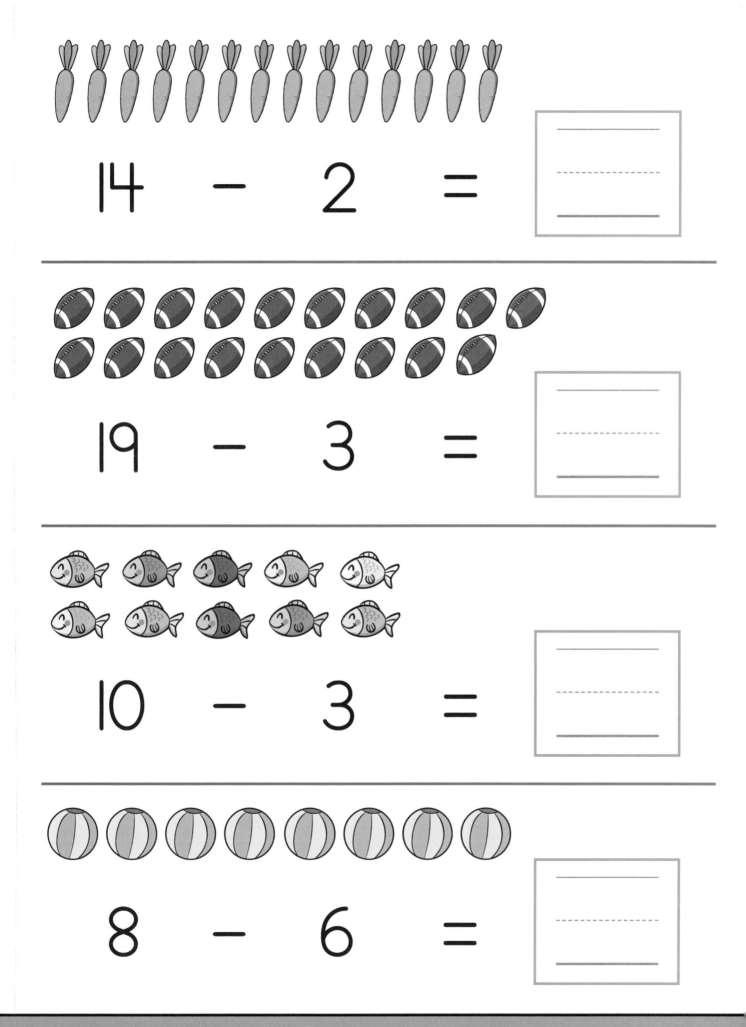

14 − 2 =

19 − 3 =

10 − 3 =

8 − 6 =

Snakes and Ladders

Work your way down each **ladder**, solving the **sums** as you go.

Circle the snake with the **highest** number.

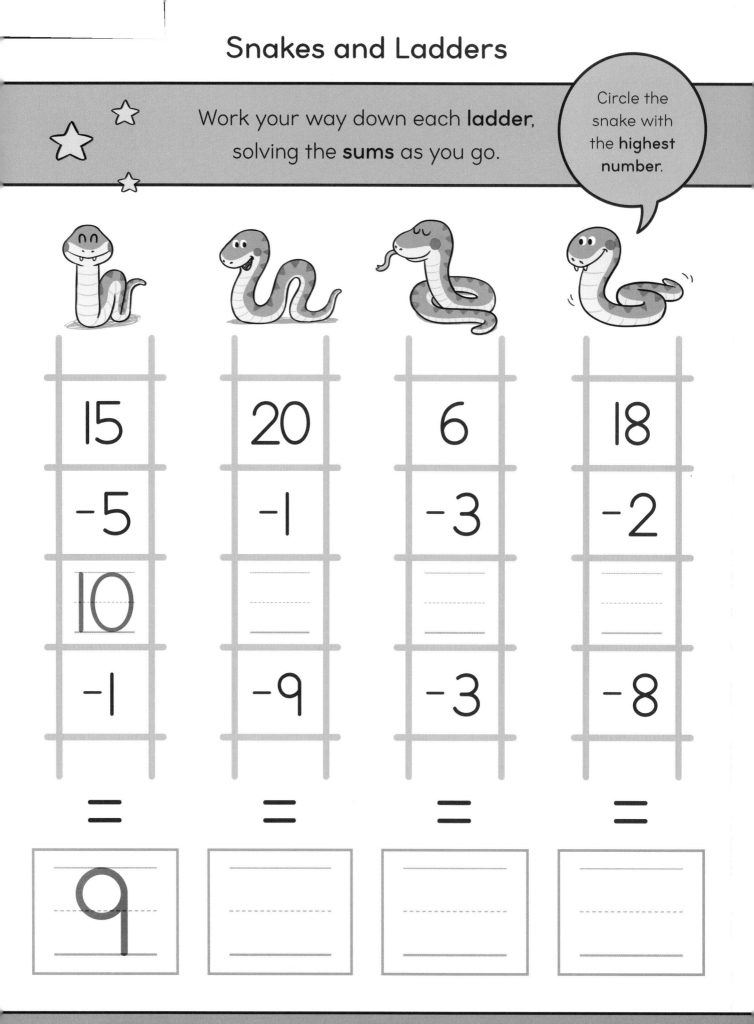

15	20	6	18
-5	-1	-3	-2
10			
-1	-9	-3	-8
=	=	=	=
9			

Subtraction Maze

Find the **sums** below. Then, **follow numbers backward** from 5 to 0 to reach downtown.

2D Shapes

Trace the **shapes**. Then, draw lines to **match** each shape with the correct label.

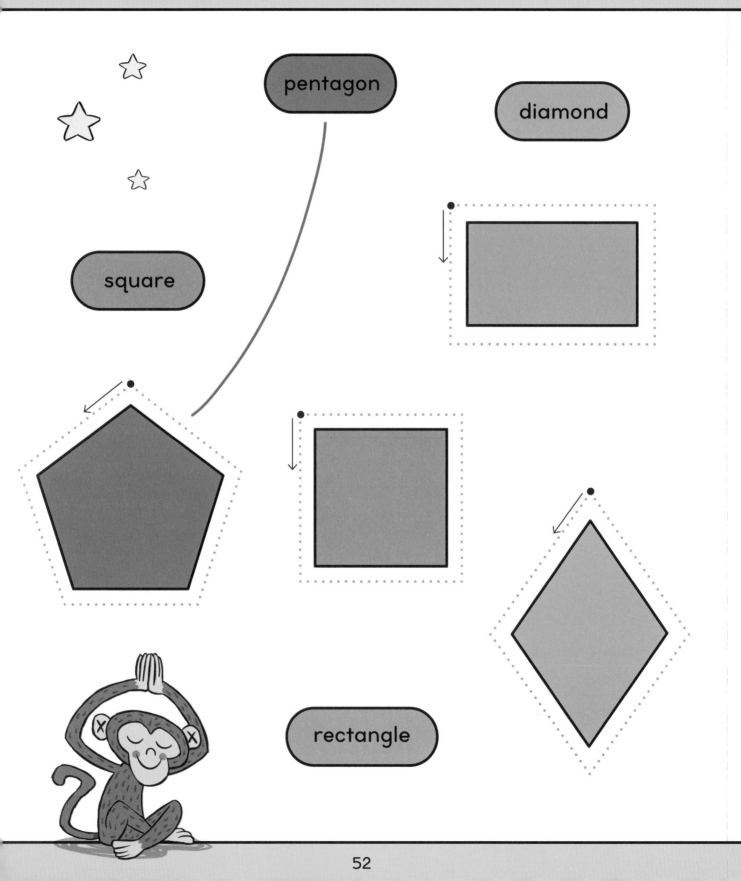

pentagon

diamond

square

rectangle

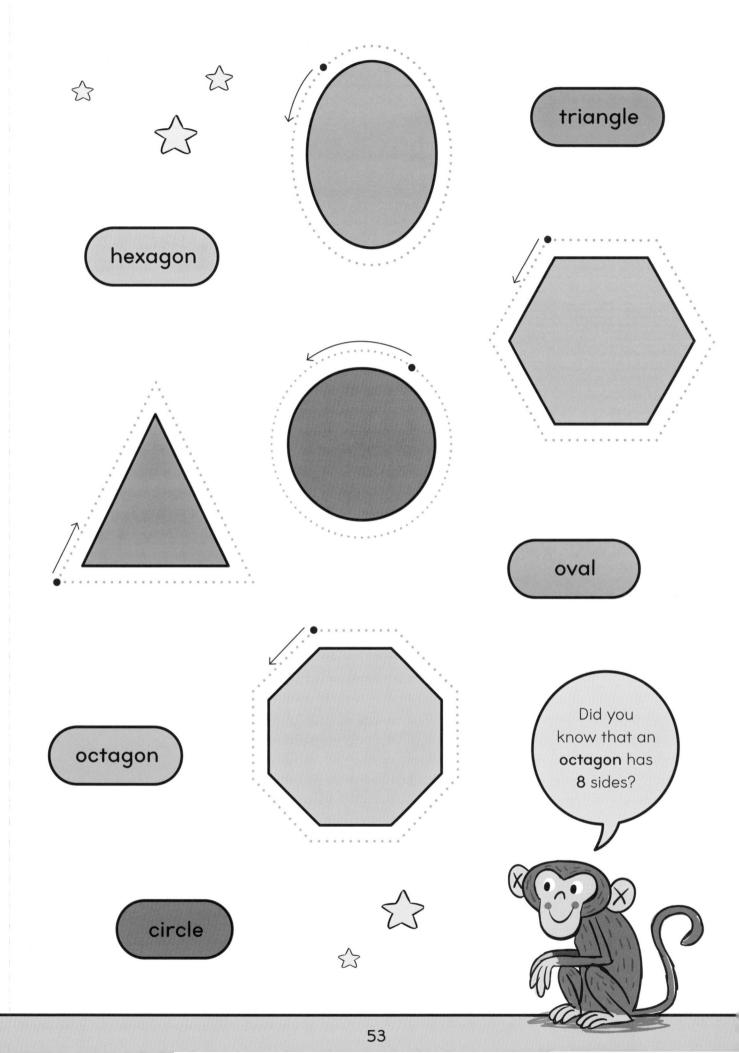

triangle

hexagon

oval

octagon

circle

Did you know that an **octagon** has 8 sides?

Counting Sides

Count how many **sides** these shapes have.

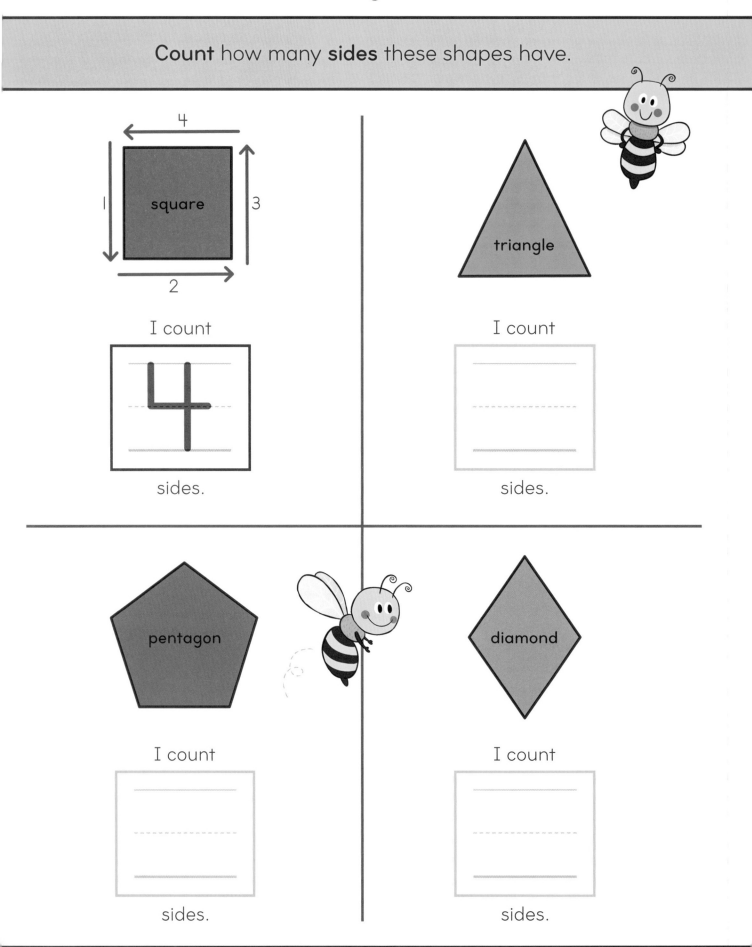

square

4
1
3
2

I count

4

sides.

triangle

I count

sides.

pentagon

I count

sides.

diamond

I count

sides.

Counting Corners

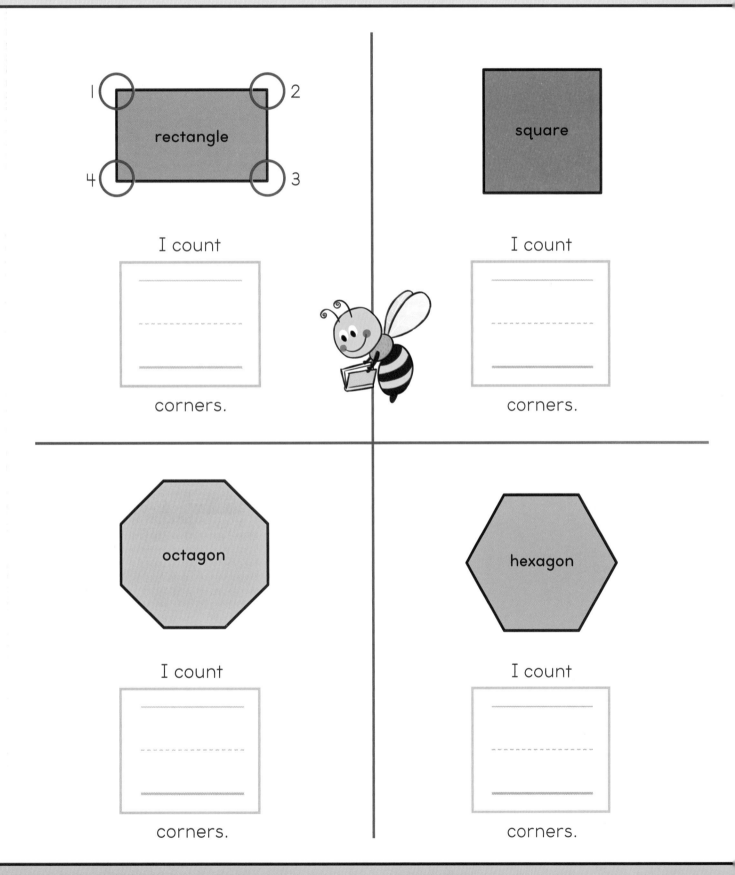

1 ○ ☐ ○ 2

rectangle

4 ○ ☐ ○ 3

I count

_____

corners.

square

I count

_____

corners.

octagon

I count

_____

corners.

hexagon

I count

_____

corners.

Shape Symmetry

Draw the other half of each **symmetrical** shape.

Something is **symmetrical** when it is the same on both sides. Place a mirror on the center lines and see what happens!

Building Shapes

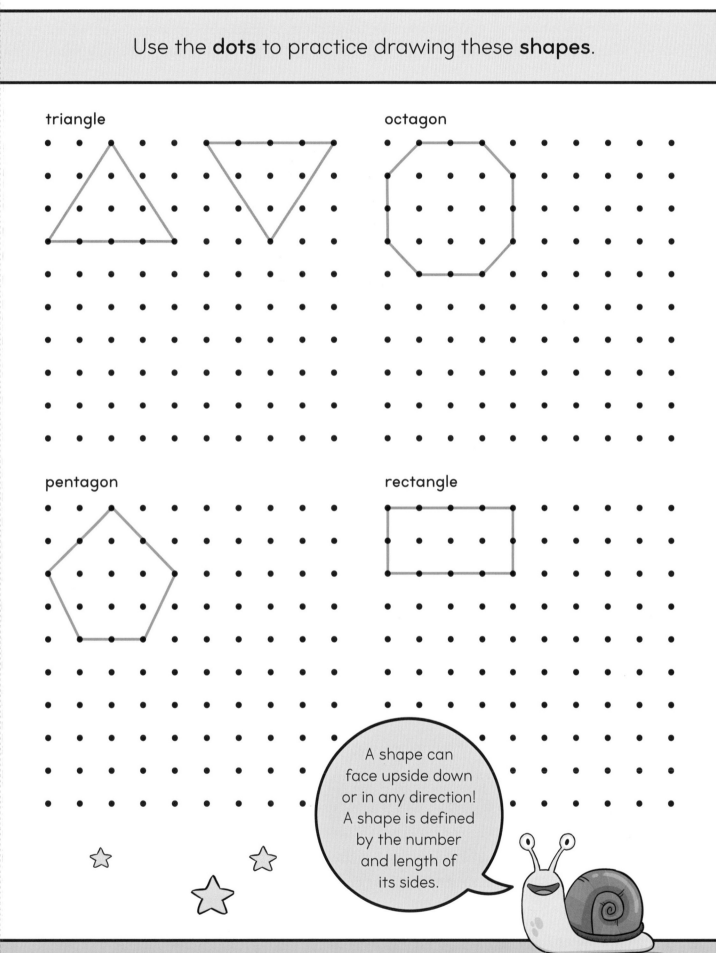

triangle

octagon

pentagon

rectangle

A shape can face upside down or in any direction! A shape is defined by the number and length of its sides.

3D Shapes

Color the **2D** shapes in blue and the **3D** shapes in red.

A 2D shape is **flat**, whereas a 3D shape is **not flat**.

sphere

triangle

rectangle

pyramid

pentagon

cylinder

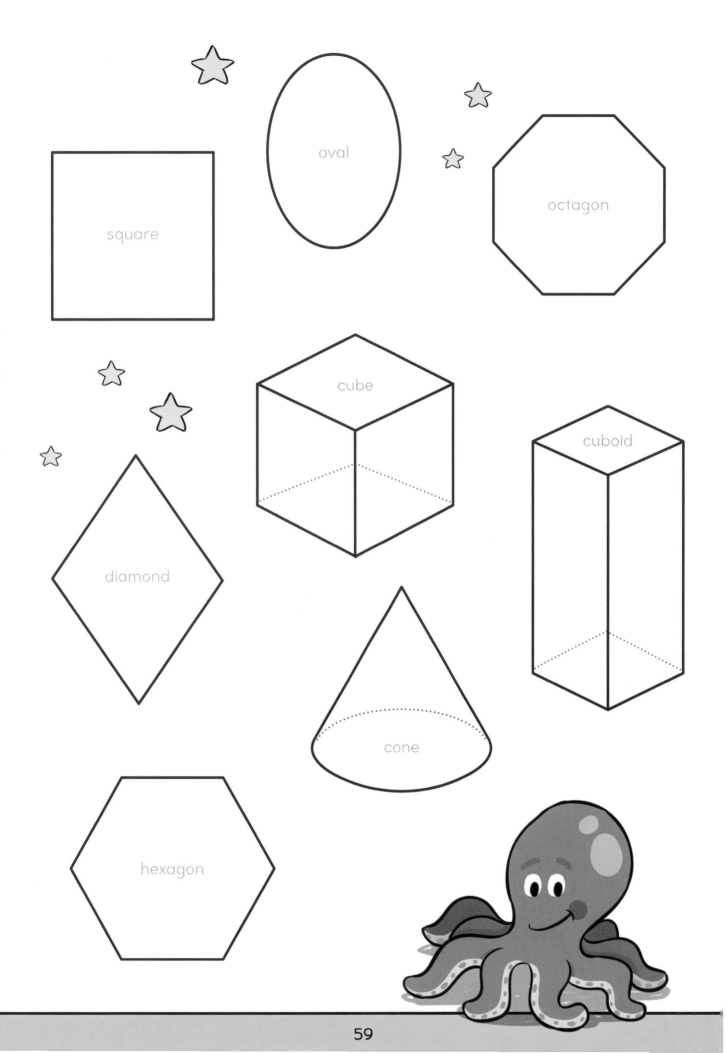

square

oval

octagon

cube

cuboid

diamond

cone

hexagon

Patterns

Study each **pattern** below and fill in the missing spaces by drawing the correct shape and its color.

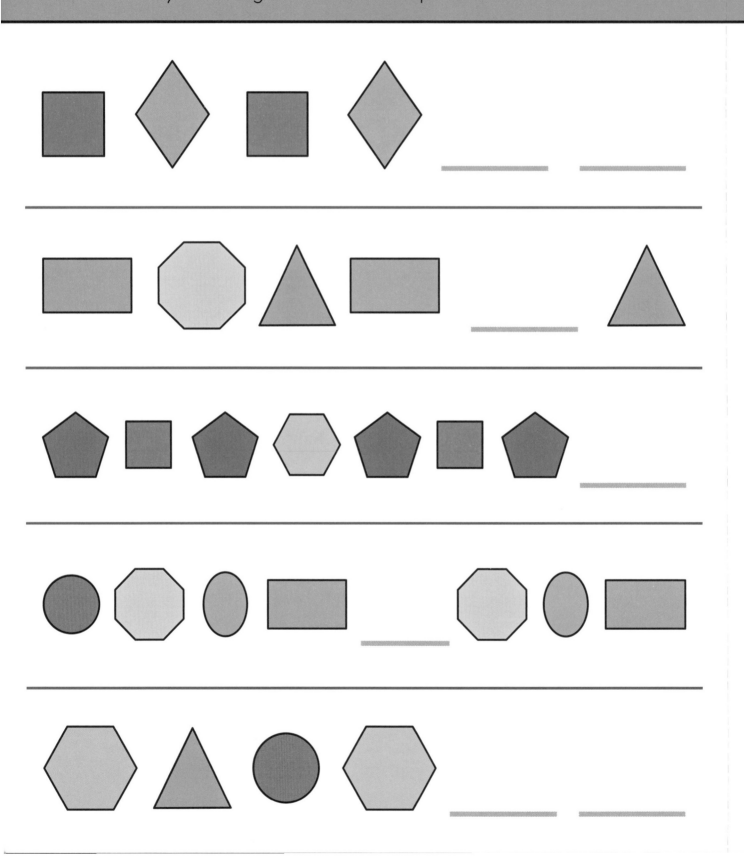

Find the Difference

Circle the picture that **does not match** the rest in each row.

Odd or Even?

even

3

✓

odd

If all the dots can be joined into pairs, the number is **even**. If there is a dot without a pair, then the number is **odd**.

even

odd

even

odd

even

odd

even

odd

even

odd

Coloring Odd and Even

Color the **even** numbers in **yellow**.
Color the **odd** numbers in **green**.

Size

Length

How **long** is each object?
Use the **ruler** and write the answer.

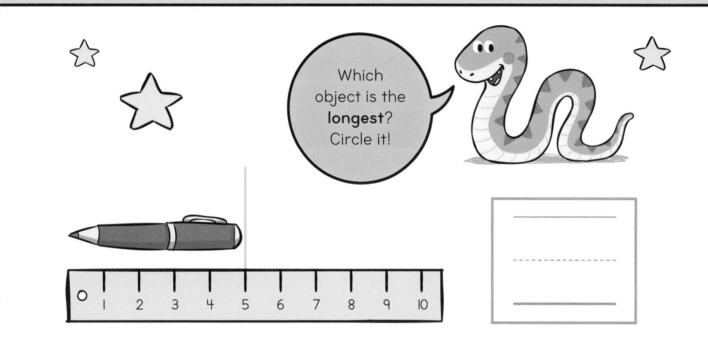

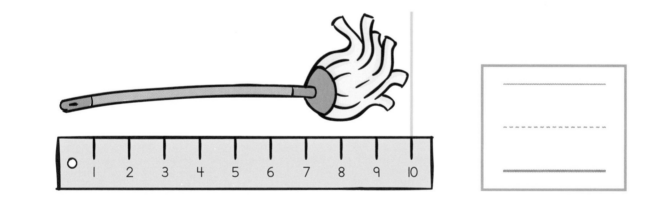

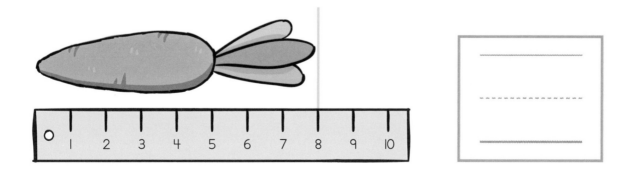

Height

How **tall** is each animal? Use the **ruler** and write the answer.

When you've finished, **circle** the **tallest** animal on the page.

Weight

The **heavier** animal will tip the scales downward!

Where Is It?

Walrus is

(inside) (outside)

the wagon.

The river runs

(under) (over)

the bridge.

Rabbit is to the

(left) (right)

of Bear as we look at them.

Dog is

(on)   (next to)

the log.

The kite is

(above)   (below)

the house.

Alligator is

(behind)   (in front of)

the tree.

Telling the Time

9 o'clock

_____ o'clock

_____ o'clock

_____ o'clock

o'clock

o'clock

o'clock

o'clock

Counting Coins

Look at the **coins** from this **piggy bank**!

penny
1 cent

nickel
5 cents

dime
10 cents

Count the money and write the **total amount**.

I count

_____
- - - - - -
_____

cents.

_____
- - - - - -
_____

cents.

_____
- - - - - -
_____

cents.

_____
- - - - - -
_____

cents.

_____
- - - - - -
_____

cents.

Counting to 100

100 one hundred

1 2 3 4 5 6

7 8 9 10 11 12

13 14 15 16 17 18

19 20 21 22 23 24

25 26 27 28 29 30

31 32 33 34 35 36

37 38 39 40 41 42

43	44	45	46	47	48
49	50	51	52	53	54
55	56	57	58	59	60
61	62	63	64	65	66
67	68	69	70	71	72
73	74	75	76	77	78
79	80	81	82	83	84
85	86	87	88	89	90
91	92	93	94	95	96
97	98	99	100		

Answers

NUMBERS 0-20
Page 15:
0, zero
1, one
2, two
3, three
4, four
5, five
6, six
7, seven
8, eight
9, nine
10, ten
11, eleven
12, twelve
13, thirteen
14, fourteen
15, fifteen
16, sixteen
17, seventeen
18, eighteen
19, nineteen
20, twenty

NUMBER ORDER
Page 16:
1, 2, 3, 4, 5, 6, 7, 8, 9, 10, 11, 12, 13, 14, 15, 16, 17, 18, 19, 20
Page 17:
20, 19, 18, 17, 16, 15, 14, 13, 12, 11, 10, 9, 8, 7, 6, 5, 4, 3, 2, 1
Page 18:
11, 12, 13, 14, 15
5, 6, 7, 8, 9
2, 3, 4, 5, 6
14, 15, 16, 17, 18
Page 19:
5, 4, 3, 2 ,1
10, 9, 8, 7, 6
5, 4, 3, 2, 1

15, 14, 13, 12, 11
20, 19, 18, 17, 16
Page 20:
3, 4
15, 16
5, 6
12, 13, 14
1, 2
16, 17
Page 21:
6, 7
10, 11
4, 5, 6
12, 13
18, 19
13, 14
8, 9
1, 2
8, 9

COUNTING
Page 22:

Page 23:
I count **19** footballs.
I count **7** apples.
I count **10** fish.
I count **20** flowers.
I count **14** carrots.
I count **17** soccer balls.

Page 24:
Yellow: 16
Page 25:
Orange: 18
Pink: 13
Purple: 11
Blue: 15
Page 26:
2, 4, 6, 8
2, 4, 6, 8, 10, 12, 14, 16, 18, 20
Page 27:
5, 10, 15, 20
Page 28:

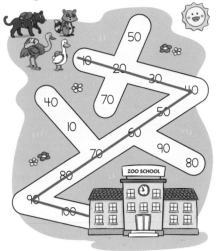

Page 29:
2, 4, 6, 8
5, 10, 15, 20
10, 20, **30**, 40
10, 12, 14, **16**, 18

COMPARING QUANTITIES
Page 30:
ice-cream cones: **9** (circle); apples: **7**; hats: **15**; logs: **16** (circle); balloons: **11** (circle); fish: **10**; Most: **logs**
Page 31:
4 pens; circle **left** group
10 fish; circle **right** group
2 party hats; circle **right** group

Page 32:
crowns: 18; carrots: 14 (circle);
oranges: 6; bananas: 3 (circle);
footballs: 19; soccer balls: 17
(circle); Fewest: **bananas**

Page 33:
12 gifts; circle **left** group
15 hats; circle **right** group
10 fish; circle **right** group

NUMBER BONDS

Page 34:
Boat, part: 1
Bananas, part: 3
Party hats, part: 2

Page 35:
Pens, part: 4
Boat, part: 1
Party hats, part: 2
Bananas, part: 3
Party hats, part: 2

Page 36:
Oranges, part: 6
Boat, part: 1
Pens, part: 4
Bananas, part: 3

Page 37:
Blank, part: 0
Oranges, part: 6
Party hats, part: 2
Bananas, part: 3

Page 38:
Balls, part: 8
Boat, part: 1
Party hats, part: 2
Shells, part: 5
Pens, part: 4

Page 39:
Blank, part: 0
Boat, part: 1
Apples, part: 7
Pens, part: 4
Bananas, part: 3

Page 40:
Blank, part: 0
Ice-cream cones, part: 9
Balls, part: 8
Apples, part: 7
Pens, part: 4

Page 41:
Party hats, part: 2
Boat, part: 1
Oranges, part: 6
Shells, part: 5
Bananas, part: 3

Page 42:
Fish, part: 10
Crowns, part: 18
Balloons, part: 11

Page 43:
Shells, part: 5
Gifts, part: 12
Footballs, part: 19
Suns, part: 13

ADDITION

Page 44:
5 + 5 = 10
5 + 15 = 20
12 + 3 = 15

Page 45:
6 + 5 = 11
13 + 5 = 18
7 + 7 = 14
10 + 9 = 19

Page 46:

Page 47:

SUBTRACTION

Page 48:
20 – 11 = 9
15 – 5 = 10

Page 49:
14 – 2 = 12
19 – 3 = 16
10 – 3 = 7
8 – 6 = 2

Page 50:
20 - 1 = 19 - 9 = 10 (circle)
6 - 3 = 3 - 3 = 0
18 - 2 = 16 - 8 = 8

Page 51:

SHAPES
Pages 52-53:

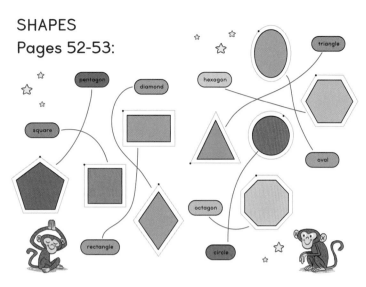

Pages 54-55:
triangle sides: **3**; pentagon sides: **5**; diamond sides: **4**; rectangle corners: **4**; square corners: **4**; octagon corners: **8**; hexagon corners: **6**

Pages 58-59:

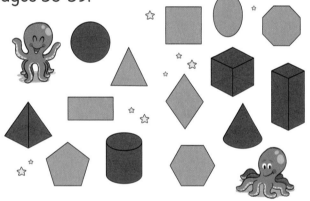

SORTING AND CLASSIFYING:
Page 60:
diamond, **square**, **diamond**
rectangle, **octagon**, triangle
pentagon, **hexagon**
rectangle, **circle**, octagon
hexagon, **triangle**, circle

Page 61:

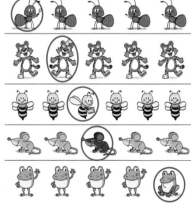

Page 62:
2: **even**; 5: **odd**; 10: **even**; 11: **odd**

Page 63:
Even numbers in yellow: **2, 4, 6, 8, 10, 12, 14, 16, 18, 20**
Odd numbers in green: **1, 3, 5, 7, 9, 11, 13, 15, 17, 19**

MEASURING:
Page 64:
rabbits: **3, 1, 4, 2**
unicorns: **4, 2, 3, 1**

Page 65:
pen: **5**
mop: **10 (longest)**
carrot: **8**

Page 66:
Goat: **5**
Giraffe: **10**
Pig: **6**
Newt: **3**

Page 67:
Elephant, Owl, Walrus

POSITIONS:
Page 68:
Walrus is **inside** the wagon.
The river runs **under** the bridge.
Rabbit is to the **right** of Bear as we look at him.

Page 69:
Dog is **next to** the log.
The kite is **above** the house.
Alligator is **in front of** the tree.

TIME:
Pages 70-71:
12 o'clock
2 o'clock
7 o'clock
6 o'clock
3 o'clock
5 o'clock
8 o'clock

MONEY:
Pages 72-74:
penny + penny + nickel = **7**
nickel + nickel = **10**
dime + nickel + penny = **16**
penny + nickel + nickel = **11**
dime + dime = **20**